This Book Belongs to

....

Using **thematic notebooks** that are adapted to specific themes such as beach holidays, weddings, or different adventures, and which include relevant images and affirmations, **brings a range of benefits.**

Here's why these notebooks can be an essential companion in your journey:

- **Focused Energy:** Helps concentrate your energy and attention on your goals.
- **Motivation:** Affirmations boost your positive thinking.
- **Clarity:** Offers space for reflection, giving insight into your goals.
- **Organization:** Place for effective planning and action.
- **Creativity:** Sparks innovative thinking with thematic elements.
- **Stress-Reducer:** Acts as an outlet for emotions, lowering stress.
- **Goal Alignment:** Helps align your actions and thoughts with your aspirations.
- **Enjoyable:** Thematic and visual elements make writing pleasant.
- **Portable:** Easy to carry at 6x9 size, allowing instant note-taking.

By channeling your focus through a thematic notebook, you are essentially directing your energy, thoughts, and actions towards your aspirations, making them a **powerful tool in personal development.**

Search for "Caroline Ina Riviera" (the author) or "Buzzing Money Books" on Amazon. You can also scan the QR code above.

Grab your thematic notebook and start your journey towards achieving your goals with a clear mind and a focused heart!

Discover the Potential of Unseen Horizons

The sea pulsates with endless possibilities, just like your inner ambitions and dreams.

Within every thought, every desire, lies the energy that fuels your life - and even money mirrors this energy.

Reaching your dream goals is not just about passion but also a clear direction, determination, and the right tools. If you desire to sharpen your vision further, enrich everyday moments, and come closer to fulfilling dreams, our 'Coloring Saving Challenge Books' will become your treasure map. They are not just books; they are companions on your journey of growth.

Ready to venture further?

Scan the QR code below and turn dreams into actionable steps. Embark on a journey across waves of new possibilities!